REPEAT AFTER ME

DATE DUE

Demco, Inc. 38-293

REPEAT AFTER ME

Poems by Bill Berkson

Watercolors by John Zurier

Published by Gallery Paule Anglim, San Francisco

Contents

Poems and Watercolors

Slow Swirl at the Edge of the Sea

Figures in trees screech;
The sun steams, the near air boggles,
Et voilá, the brooding nimbus.

Death, real death, it's an Old World custom,
A certain semblance of knowing
What's what, without which nothing works.

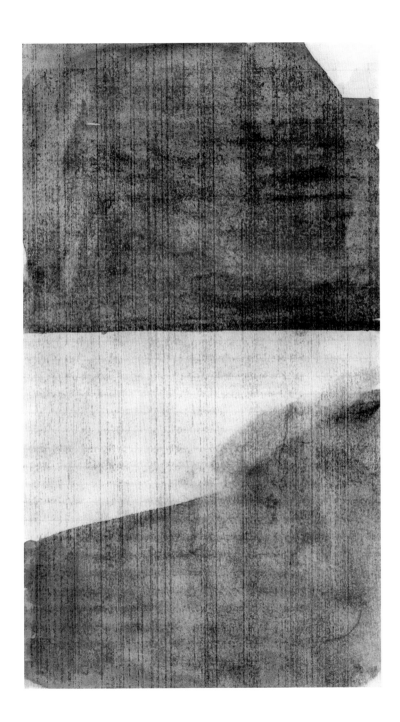

Earth's Debit

Solar photons and ergs
       conspire upheaval
             in someone's air
                       no smile but hands
                on the passenger side
       worked up
                to have had a career
            a brilliance so severe
another compass rose, its leavings left for dead
       at best and/or mummified

Lady Air

The meaning of guitar practice
Slips between pine needles
A bird that thin
To the tune of "Start Me Up"

Rubrics of screen porch and firefly
Embolden the effort

All words are prophetic
Bare the thread, swallow the cloud
Reflected glory drives off
Leaving the original in demand

Repeat after me

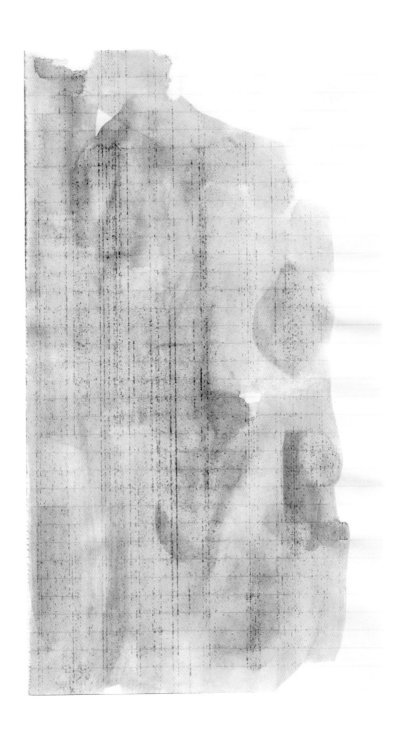

Decal

Coffee to go in either hand
Shady exit down the spa steps
Indentured tulip morning engine zenith

A butterfly speeds off
Weary of these flats
Where palm trees pose and the children push

Macabre distinctions all told
Tragic as a near miss for indifference sake
The moonlit frigate sequestered on a reef

She'll have the silver taken at one of her lengths
Turn the air to proper then
Make mine magnolia

The One God

Once heaven was just a boy and a girl
And a path to the beach.
That was before the rooms were gutted and you learned

How to exhibit bereavement
Would earn your weight in brimming
Moon lagers.

Literally, "the bee's knees."
The shoulders of Roland de Smoke
Cuddle two abreast on a tray.

While air lasts, cities also die, old gasbags
With quilted manners, prepuce because the English
Taste in pictures slackened.

Then again, despite the poison crumbs,
The two just walk on tiptoes out of doors,
Pressing along the keen incline.

What will happen, what to say
If and when the first door opens, the wings
Flutter in turn as nights subside?

In Königsberg, However

Pardon the insult, move the herd
Nothing a guy can't do, ergo study
Harder if you are found wanting

No secret there
Part conniption, enter fate
Slow bag of viscous matter on a string

Plausible entities trade robes
Bad physics squeaks by
To cater excess of air

A favorite of the colors
This side of the angels
Under low aesthetic skies

Dress Trope

Critics should wear
      white jackets like
  lab technicians;
          curators, zoo
     keepers' caps;
 and art historians,
           lead aprons
to protect them from
     impending
  radiant fact.

Sea Breeze

The flesh is sad, alas! and I've read all the books.
To flee! Out there! I sense some birds are drunk
From reeling amid unknown foam and skies!
Nothing, no old gardens reflected in eyes,
Will restrain this heart so immersed in the sea
O nights! nor the barren clarity of my lamp
On the blank paper, its white defense,
And not my young wife nursing her babe.
I'll leave. Steamer rocking your spars,
Weigh anchor for some exotic clime!

Ennui, unhinged by cruel hopes,
Still believes in handkerchiefs, the ultimate goodbye!
And perhaps the masts, inviting storms,
Are those a wind will send keeling onto wrecks
Lost, with no masts, no masts, no fertile atoll shore....
But, O my heart, listen to the sailors' song!

after Stéphane Mallarmé, "Brise Marine"

The Gift of the Poem

I bring you the child of Idumaean night!
Black, with pale and bloody wing, all feathers plucked,
Through glass inflamed by spices and gold,
Through frosted panes, gloomy still, alas!
Dawn threw itself on the angelic lamp,
O palms! And when it showed its relic
To this father venturing his inimical smile,
The sterile blue solitude quaked.
O cradle, with your baby girl and the innocence
Of your cold feet, receive this horrid birth;
And with a voice resonant of harpsichord and viol,
Will your withered finger press the breast
Whence in sibylline whiteness the woman flows
For lips deprived in virgin azure air?

after Stéphane Mallarmé, "Don de Poéme"

Two Russian Poems

for Kate Sutton

Poem

Stars rushed onward. Cliffs bathed themselves in the sea.
Salt spray blinded, and tears dried up.
The bedrooms darkened. Thoughts rushed.
The Sphinx nodded to Sahara's whispers.

Candles swam, and it seemed the blood ran cold
Inside the Colossus. Lips swelled
Into the desert's slow blue smile.
As tides turned, night declined.

Moroccan breezes stirred the sea.
Simoon howled. Archangel snored in its snows.
Candles swam. Rough draft of "The Prophet"
Dried, and day glimmered over the Ganges.

after Boris Pasternak

The Prophet

Parched with spiritual thirst, I crossed
An endless desert sunk in gloom,
And a six-winged seraph came
To the crossroads where I stood lost.
Fingers light as dreams he laid
Upon my lids; my eyes sprung open
And started like a wary eaglet's.
He put his fingers to my ears
And they rang, filling with a thunderous roar:
And I heard the shuddering of the spheres,
And the proud horn of the angels' flight,
And beasts moving under the sea,
And the heady surge of the vine;
And he pressed open my lips,
And rooted out this shameful tongue of mine,
Fluent in vanity and lies;
And with his bloody hand he slapped
Between my frozen lips the wily serpent's sting;
And his sword split my breast;
And my pounding heart leaped up;
And a glowing livid coal he pressed
Into the hollow of the wound.
There in the desert I lay as if dead,
And the Voice called out, saying:
"Rise, Prophet, and see and hear,
And let my Will be known to all,
And passing over lands and seas,
Burn their hearts with my fiery Word."

after Alexander Pushkin [1827]

The Cloud of Knowing

Peri hupsus, the poetry of hype?

"From then on, I knew
I could sell people anything,"

the artist lately known as
Jeff Koons beamed,

his juvenilia success parading
baked goods door to door.

And for those who can't or won't—
it hadn't occurred to them,

nor had "anything" ever come their way.

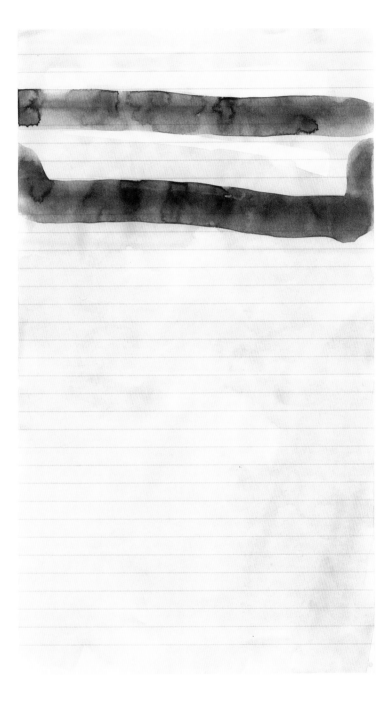

With Impunity

Light enters the retina by way of the surge
Of heavy morning traffic down Upper Market

The province, the region, the sect
The zone of last clouds in which is spotted the Final Face

Trickle in culverts beyond
– "This call ends now" –

A bird suffocates before you know it
Eurasia of the Abstract, Russian poetry edgy

And green like a chambray work shirt
Snippets in a mineshaft, so dispersed, hurtful

Anhedonia

"You must understand, it is difficult for me to die."
"And it is easy for us to go on living?"
—Bukharin/ Stalin, Plenum of the Central Committee, 1937

Or maybe the other way around;
I've lost the thread:
Something about Evil Days, Evil Ways,

Business as usual,
The kids, their schools
And the Infernal Machine.

Difficult it is, regardless of what
Is said or put to writing
In the end.

Say we do as we please — tacit approval
Of a faulty transcription, sentence
Taken down, in a kind of rapture.

Premises of the Solstice

Eastern sky
at morning, all

peaches and cream –
streaks

of late-night promise
astride the dome

of heaven,
casually fulfilled.

December 21, 2010

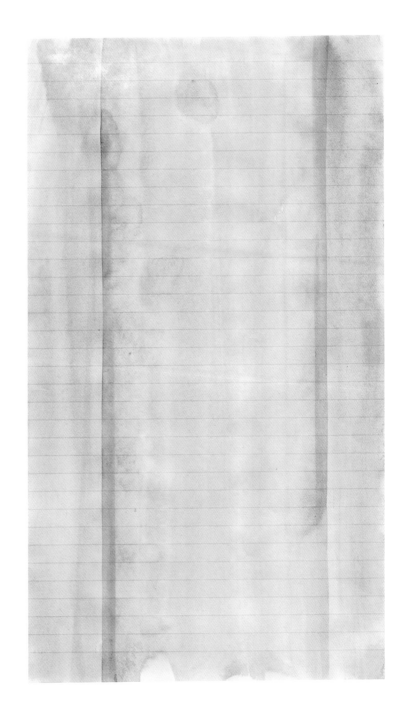

Birthday Greetings

after François de La Rochefoucauld

To you,
one of very few
good excuses
ever given
for life on Earth.

List of plates

(all works watercolor on Japanese paper, 9 $^7/_8$ x 5 $^{11}/_{16}$ inches)

Born in New York in 1939, **Bill Berkson** is a poet and critic who has lived in Northern California since the early 1970s. He is Professor Emeritus at the San Francisco Art Institute, where he taught art history and literature for many years. A corresponding editor for *Art in America*, he has contributed to such other journals as *Artforum*, *Aperture* and *artcritical.com*. His most recent books include *Portrait and Dream: New & Selected Poems*; *BILL*, a words-and-images collaboration with Colter Jacobsen; *Lady Air*; *Not an Exit* with drawings by Léonie Guyer; a new collection of his art writings, *For the Ordinary Artist*; and *Parties du corps*, a selection of his poetry in French translation. He was the 2006 Distinguished Mellon Fellow at the Skowhegan School of Painting and Sculpture and received the 2008 Goldie for Literature from the San Francisco *Bay Guardian*. *Portrait and Dream* won the Balcones Prize for Best Poetry Book of 2010.

Born in Santa Monica in 1956, **John Zurier** is a painter who has lived in Berkeley since 1974. He is currently Eminent Adjunct Professor at California College of the Arts in San Francisco, where he teaches in the Graduate Program in Fine Arts and the undergraduate Painting/Drawing Program. His work was shown in the California Biennial at the Orange County Museum of Art (2010-2011); and at the Indianapolis Museum of Contemporary Art (2010), UC Berkeley Art Museum (2009), The 7th Gwangju Biennial, Gwangju, South Korea (2008); Colby College Museum of Art, Waterville, Maine (2007); Kettle's Yard, Cambridge, England (2003); and the Whitney Biennial (2002), among others. His work is represented by Gallery Paule Anglim, San Francisco; and Peter Blum Gallery, New York. He was awarded a John Simon Guggenheim Fellowship in 2010.

Also by Bill Berkson

Versions of some of the poems in this book have appeared
in *Lady Air* (Perdika Press, 2010), *Peaches and Bats,
Shampoo, OnandOnScreen, Live Mag, Brown Literary
Review, Try, Gerry Mulligan* and *Exquisite Corpse Annual.*

"Decal" appeared as Woodland Pattern Center broadside
in 2009.

"Andehonia" and "Premises of the Solstice" were
published in a small chapbook, *Darkness and Light*, by
Peter Anderson's Verna Press, 2011.

Published by
Gallery Paule Anglim
14 Geary Street
San Francisco, CA 94108
www.gallerypauleanglim.com

Distributed by
Small Press Distribution
1341 Seventh Street
Berkeley, CA 94710-1403
www.spdbooks.org
orders@spdbooks.org

Designed by Nina Hubbs Zurier

500 copies printed in California, 2011
ISBN 978-0-615-53603-3